Selected from
THE JOY LUCK CLUB

AMY TAN

WRITERS' VOICES
New Readers Press

Selection: From THE JOY LUCK CLUB by AMY TAN.
Copyright © 1989 by Amy Tan. Reprinted by permission of
Putnam Publishing Group.

Additional material
Copyright © 1992
New Readers Press
U.S. Publishing Division of Laubach Literacy International
Box 131, Syracuse, New York 13210-0131

All rights reserved. No part of this book may be reproduced
or transmitted in any form or by any means, electronic or
mechanical, including photocopying, recording, or by any
information storage and retrieval system, without permission
in writing from the publisher.

Printed in the United States of America

10 9 8 7 6 5 4

First printing: May 1992

ISBN 0-929631-51-X

The words "Writers' Voices" are a trademark of
New Readers Press

Cover designed by Paul Davis Studio
Interior designed by Jules Perimutter, Off-Broadway Graphics

Acknowledgments

We gratefully acknowledge the generous support of the following foundations and corporations that made the publication of WRITERS' VOICES and NEW WRITERS' VOICES possible: An anonymous foundation; The Vincent Astor Foundation; Exxon Corporation; Knight Foundation; Scripps Howard Foundation; Uris Brothers Foundation and H.W. Wilson Foundation.

This book could not have been realized without the kind and generous cooperation of the author, Amy Tan, her editor, Faith Sale, and her publisher, The Putnam Publishing Group. Thanks to Christopher K. Sheridan, permissions department.

We deeply appreciate the contributions of the following suppliers: Cam Steel Rule Die Works Inc. (steel cutting die for display); Canadian Forest Products, Ltd. (text stock); Creative Graphics Inc. (text typesetting); Westvaco Corporation (cover stock); MCUSA (display header); Delta Corrugated Container (corrugated display); Stevenson Photo Color Company (cover color separations); Coral Graphic Services Inc. (cover printing) and R.R. Donnelley & Sons Company (text printing and binding).

Our thanks to Paul Davis Studio and Myrna Davis, Paul Davis, Lisa Mazur, Chalkley Calderwood and Alex Ginns for their inspired design of the covers of these books. Thanks also to Jules Perlmutter for his sensitive design of the interior of this book. Thanks also to AnnLouise Burns for design of maps.

Contents

✿

Note to the Reader	6
About the Selections from *The Joy Luck Club*	10
Selected from *The Joy Luck Club*, by Amy Tan	13
Maps of Places Mentioned in the Selections	46
Questions for the Reader	47
Glossary	52
About Amy Tan	53
About Modern China	55
About Mah Jong	61
Chronology of Events	62

Note to the Reader

✿

The book *The Joy Luck Club* by Amy Tan is a story about four Chinese women and their Chinese-American adult daughters. The mothers all came to America in the 1940s, when there was a revolution in China.

In America, the women raise their families. Their daughters, having grown up in America, hold very different ideas from their mothers about what a good life means. Yet the mothers and daughters also have ties that cannot be broken.

Every writer has a special voice. That is why we call our series *Writers' Voices*. We chose *The Joy Luck Club* because Amy Tan's voice can be clearly heard as she tells about these mothers and daughters.

In choosing parts from the book, we selected the story of one of the mothers and her daughter—Suyuan Woo and Jing-mei "June" Woo.

Our book has several different chapters in

addition to the selections themselves. They provide background information that can help you in understanding the selections. You may choose to read some or all of these chapters before or after reading the selections.

Reading "About the Selections from *The Joy Luck Club*" on page 10 will help you begin thinking about the characters and the setting of the story.

- If you would like more information about China and its history, look at the chapter called "About Modern China" on page 55.
- If you would like to get an overview of the events in China that take place at the same time as the story, look at the chapter called "Chronology of Events" on page 62.
- If you would like more information on mah jong, the game the women play, look at the chapter called "About Mah Jong" on page 61.
- Many readers enjoy finding out about the person who wrote the story. Sometimes this information will give you more insight into the story. You can learn more about Amy Tan in the chapter "About Amy Tan" on page 53.

If you are a new reader, you may want to have this book read aloud to you, perhaps more than once. Even if you are a more experienced reader, you may enjoy hearing it read aloud before reading it silently to yourself.

We encourage you to read *actively*. Here are some things you can do.

Before Reading

- Read the front and back covers of the book, and look at the cover illustration. Ask yourself what you expect the book to be about.
- Think about why you want to read this book. Maybe you know someone whose family came from China. Maybe you want to read something about relationships between mothers and daughters.
- Look at the Contents page. Find the page with a map of where the story takes place. Decide what you want to read and in what order.

During Reading

- There may be words that are difficult to read. Keep reading to see if the meaning becomes clear. If it doesn't, ask someone for the word. Some of the Chinese words are explained in

the Glossary on page 52. Or look up the words in a dictionary.
- Ask yourself questions as you read. For example, how do children's thoughts and feelings about their parents change when they understand more about their pasts?

After Reading

- Think about what you have read. Did you identify with Jing-mei or Suyuan? Did you see any of your own family experiences in a new light?
- Talk with others about your thoughts.
- Try some of the questions and activities in "Questions for the Reader" on page 47. They are meant to help you discover more about what you have read and how it relates to you.

The editors of *Writers' Voices* hope you will write to us. We want to know your thoughts about our books.

About the Selections from The Joy Luck Club

✿

The book *The Joy Luck Club* contains stories about Chinese mothers and their Chinese-American daughters who live in San Francisco, California. These selections are about Jing-mei "June" Woo and her mother, Suyuan Woo.

When the story begins, Suyuan Woo has just died. Jing-mei's father, Canning Woo, asks Jing-mei to take her mother's place at the regular meetings of the Joy Luck Club. Each week, four Chinese women meet to talk, eat and play mah jong. (Mah jong is a game from Asia. For more information on mah jong, see page 61.)

Jing-mei then remembers the story her mother told her about how she started a Joy Luck Club in China in 1944, years before she came to the United States. At the time, Suyuan was married to an officer in the army of the Kuomintang, the Chinese Nationalist Party. They were fighting a war against the Japanese.

During the war, people like Suyuan came from all over China to the city of Kweilin. They came because they thought they would be safe there, away from the fighting. Kweilin was known for its beautiful mountains, caves and trees. But with the war going on, there was a food shortage. Money was worthless. Bombing could be heard all around.

To keep her spirits up, Suyuan started a mah jong group with three other young women who had lost everything in the war. They named the group the Joy Luck Club because the women hoped that, even though times were so bad, they could become happy and lucky again.

At the Joy Luck Club, the women played mah jong for money and served special foods that they believed would bring them good luck. They called them *dyansyin* foods. They laughed, talked and hoped for better times.

To the American-born Jing-mei, her mother's story seems unreal, like a fairy tale. But as she grows older, she learns more about her mother's past. This new information makes the story real to Jing-mei, but the truth is hard to accept.

Jing-mei learns of the many hardships and sorrows her mother endured during the war. She learns how Suyuan lost her first husband, remarried and came to the United States.

When Suyuan came to San Francisco in 1949,

she started the same kind of club for other women war refugees. After suffering through the war, they needed the hope that the Joy Luck Club could bring. The women in the club became Suyuan's best friends. In the selections, Jing-mei calls these women her "aunties."

When Jing-mei takes her mother's place at the Joy Luck Club, her aunties tell her more about her mother. Jing-mei begins to understand the hopes and fears of these Chinese women for their daughters. The aunties start Jing-mei on a quest that will make her confront and understand her Chinese roots.

These selections tell two main stories. One is the story of Jing-mei and her feelings about her mother. The other is the story of Suyuan and her experiences in China during the war.

The stories are told through the eyes of different people. Most of the story selected here is told in Jing-mei's voice. But from pages 16 to 27, Jing-mei's mother tells about China. And from pages 39 to 43, the story is told from Jing-mei's father's point of view.

Perhaps this story will make you think about a parent's or relative's experience in a different way. Maybe it will make you think about how your heritage shapes you in ways you did not expect.

Selected from

THE JOY LUCK CLUB

My father has asked me to be the fourth corner at the Joy Luck Club. I am to replace my mother, whose seat at the mah jong table has been empty since she died two months ago. My father thinks she was killed by her own thoughts.

"She had a new idea inside her head," said my father. "But before it could come out of her mouth, the thought grew too big and burst. It must have been a very bad idea."

The doctor said she died of a cerebral

aneurysm. And her friends at the Joy Luck Club said she died just like a rabbit: quickly and with unfinished business left behind. My mother was supposed to host the next meeting of the Joy Luck Club.

The week before she died, she called me, full of pride, full of life: "Auntie Lin cooked red bean soup for Joy Luck. I'm going to cook black sesame-seed soup."

"Don't show off," I said.

"It's not showoff." She said the two soups were almost the same, *chabuduo*. Or maybe she said *butong*, not the same thing at all. It was one of those Chinese expressions that means the better half of mixed intentions. I can never remember things I didn't understand in the first place.

My mother started the San Francisco version of the Joy Luck Club in 1949, two years before I was born. This was the year my mother and father left China with one stiff leather trunk filled only with fancy silk dresses. There was no time to pack anything else, my mother had explained to my father after they boarded the boat. Still his hands swam frantically between the slippery silks, looking for his cotton shirts and wool pants.

When they arrived in San Francisco, my father made her hide those shiny clothes. She wore the same brown-checked Chinese dress until the Refugee Welcome Society gave her two hand-me-down dresses, all too large in sizes for American women. The society was composed of a group of white-haired American missionary ladies from the First Chinese Baptist Church. And because of their gifts, my parents could not refuse their invitation to join the church. Nor could they ignore the old ladies' practical advice to improve their English through Bible study class on Wednesday nights and, later, through choir practice on Saturday mornings. This was how my parents met the Hsus, the Jongs, and the St. Clairs. My mother could sense that the women of these families also had unspeakable tragedies they had left behind in China and hopes they couldn't begin to express in their fragile English. Or at least, my mother recognized the numbness in these women's faces. And she saw how quickly their eyes moved when she told them her idea for the Joy Luck Club.

Joy Luck was an idea my mother remembered

from the days of her first marriage in Kweilin, before the Japanese came. That's why I think of Joy Luck as her Kweilin story. It was the story she would always tell me when she was bored, when there was nothing to do, when every bowl had been washed and the Formica table had been wiped down twice, when my father sat reading the newspaper and smoking one Pall Mall cigarette after another, a warning not to disturb him. This is when my mother would take out a box of old ski sweaters sent to us by unseen relatives from Vancouver. She would snip the bottom of a sweater and pull out a kinky thread of yarn, anchoring it to a piece of cardboard. And as she began to roll with one sweeping rhythm, she would start her story. Over the years, she told me the same story, except for the ending, which grew darker, casting long shadows into her life, and eventually into mine.

"I dreamed about Kweilin before I ever saw it," my mother began, speaking Chinese. "I dreamed of jagged peaks lining a curving river, with magic moss greening the banks. At the tops of these peaks were white mists. And if you could float down this river and eat the moss for food, you would be strong enough to climb the peak. If you slipped, you would only fall into a bed of soft moss and laugh. And once you reached the top, you would be able to see everything and feel such happiness it would be enough to never have worries in your life ever again.

"In China, everybody dreamed about Kweilin. And when I arrived, I realized how shabby my dreams were, how poor my thoughts. When I saw the hills, I laughed and shuddered at the same time. The peaks looked like giant fried fish heads trying to jump out of a vat of oil. Behind each hill, I could see shadows of another fish, and then another and another. And then the clouds would move just a little and the hills would suddenly become monstrous elephants marching slowly toward me! Can you see this? And at the root of the hill were secret caves. Inside grew hanging rock gardens in the shapes and colors of cabbage, winter melons, turnips, and onions. These were things so strange and beautiful you can't ever imagine them.

"But I didn't come to Kweilin to see how beautiful it was. The man who was my husband brought me and our two babies to Kweilin because he thought we would be safe. He was an officer with the Kuomintang, and after he put us down in a small room in a two-story house, he went off to the northwest, to Chungking.

"We knew the Japanese were winning, even when the newspapers said they were not. Every day, every hour, thousands of people poured into the city, crowding the sidewalks, looking for places to live. They came from the East, West, North, and South. They were rich and poor, Shanghainese, Cantonese, northerners, and not just Chinese, but foreigners and missionaries of every religion. And there was, of course, the Kuomintang and their army officers who thought they were top level to everyone else.

"We were a city of leftovers mixed together. If it hadn't been for the Japanese, there would have been plenty of reason for fighting to break out among these different people. Can you see it? Shanghai people with north-water peasants, bankers with barbers, rickshaw pullers with Burma refugees. Everybody looked down on someone else. It didn't matter that everybody shared the same sidewalk to spit on and suffered the same fast-moving diarrhea. We all had the same stink, but everybody complained someone else smelled the worst. Me? Oh, I hated the American air force officers who said habba-habba sounds to make my face turn red. But the worst were the northern peasants who emptied their noses into their hands and pushed people around and gave everybody their dirty diseases.

"So you can see how quickly Kweilin lost its beauty for me. I no longer climbed the peaks to say, How lovely are these hills! I only wondered which hills the Japanese had reached. I sat in the dark corners of my house with a baby under each arm, waiting with nervous feet. When the sirens cried out to warn us of bombers, my neighbors and I jumped to our feet and scurried to the deep caves to hide like wild animals. But you can't stay in the dark for so long. Something inside of you starts to fade and you become like a starving person, crazy-hungry for light. Outside I could hear the bombing. Boom! Boom! And then the sound of raining rocks. And inside I was no longer hungry for the cabbage or the turnips of the hanging rock garden. I could only see the dripping bowels of an ancient hill that might collapse on top of me. Can you imagine how it is, to want to be neither inside nor outside, to want to be nowhere and disappear?

"So when the bombing sounds grew farther away, we would come back out like newborn kittens scratching our way back to the city. And always, I would be amazed to find the hills against the burning sky had not been torn apart.

"I thought up Joy Luck on a summer night that was so hot even the moths fainted to the ground, their wings were so heavy with the damp heat. Every place was so crowded there was no room for fresh air. Unbearable smells from the sewers rose up to my second-story window and the stink had nowhere else to go but into my nose. At all hours of the night and day, I heard screaming sounds. I didn't know if it was a peasant slitting the throat of a runaway pig or an officer beating a half-dead peasant for lying in his way on the sidewalk. I didn't go to the window to find out. What use would it have been? And that's when I thought I needed something to do to help me move.

"My idea was to have a gathering of four women, one for each corner of my mah jong table. I knew which women I wanted to ask. They were all young like me, with wishful faces. One was an army officer's wife, like myself. Another was a girl with very fine manners from a rich family in Shanghai. She had escaped with only a little money. And there was a girl from Nanking who had the blackest hair I have ever seen. She came from a low-class family, but she was pretty and pleasant and had married well, to an old man who died and left her with a better life.

"Each week one of us would host a party to raise money and to raise our spirits. The hostess had to serve special *dyansyin* foods to bring good fortune of all kinds—dumplings shaped like silver money ingots, long rice noodles for long life, boiled peanuts for conceiving sons, and of course, many good-luck oranges for a plentiful, sweet life.

"What fine food we treated ourselves to with our meager allowances! We didn't notice that the dumplings were stuffed mostly with stringy squash and that the oranges were spotted with wormy holes. We ate sparingly, not as if we didn't have enough, but to protest how we could not eat another bite, we had already bloated ourselves from earlier in the day. We knew we had luxuries few people could afford. We were the lucky ones.

"After filling our stomachs, we would then fill a bowl with money and put it where everyone could see. Then we would sit down at the mah jong table. My table was from my family and was of a very fragrant red wood, not what you call rosewood, but *hong mu*, which is so fine there's no English word for it. The table had a very thick pad, so that when the mah jong *pai* were spilled onto the table the only sound was of ivory tiles washing against one another.

"Once we started to play, nobody could speak, except to say *'Pung!'* or *'Chr!'* when taking a tile. We had to play with seriousness and think of nothing else but adding to our happiness through winning. But after sixteen rounds, we would again feast, this time to celebrate our good fortune. And then we would talk into the night until the morning, saying stories about good times in the past and good times yet to come.

"Oh, what good stories! Stories spilling out all over the place! We almost laughed to death. A rooster that ran into the house screeching on top of dinner bowls, the same bowls that held him quietly in pieces the next day! And one about a girl who wrote love letters for two friends who loved the same man. And a silly foreign lady who fainted on a toilet when firecrackers went off next to her.

"People thought we were wrong to serve banquets every week while many people in the city were starving, eating rats and, later, the garbage that the poorest rats used to feed on. Others thought we were possessed by demons—to celebrate when even within our own families we had lost generations, had lost homes and fortunes, and were separated, husband from wife, brother from sister, daughter from mother. Hnnnh! How could we laugh, people asked.

"It's not that we had no heart or eyes for pain. We were all afraid. We all had our miseries. But to despair was to wish back for something already lost. Or to prolong what was already unbearable. How much can you wish for a favorite warm coat that hangs in the closet of a house that burned down with your mother and father inside of it? How long can you see in your mind arms and legs hanging from telephone wires and starving dogs running down the streets with half-chewed hands dangling from their jaws? What was worse, we asked among ourselves, to sit and wait for our own deaths with proper somber faces? Or to choose our own happiness?

"So we decided to hold parties and pretend each week had become the new year. Each week we could forget past wrongs done to us. We weren't allowed to think a bad thought. We feasted, we laughed, we played games, lost and won, we told the best stories. And each week, we could hope to be lucky. That hope was our only joy. And that's how we came to call our little parties Joy Luck."

My mother used to end the story on a happy note, bragging about her skill at the game. "I won many times and was so lucky the others teased that I had learned the trick of a clever thief," she said. "I won tens of thousands of *yuan*. But I wasn't rich. No. By then paper money had become worthless. Even toilet paper was worth more. And that made us laugh harder, to think a thousand-*yuan* note wasn't even good enough to rub on our bottoms."

I never thought my mother's Kweilin story was anything but a Chinese fairy tale. The endings always changed. Sometimes she said she used that worthless thousand-*yuan* note to buy a half-cup of rice. She turned that rice into a pot of porridge. She traded that gruel for two feet from a pig. Those two feet became six eggs, those eggs six chickens. The story always grew and grew.

And then one evening, after I had begged her to buy me a transistor radio, after she refused and I had sulked in silence for an hour, she said,

"Why do you think you are missing something you never had?" And then she told me a completely different ending to the story.

"An army officer came to my house early one morning," she said, "and told me to go quickly to my husband in Chungking. And I knew he was telling me to run away from Kweilin. I knew what happened to officers and their families when the Japanese arrived. How could I go? There were no trains leaving Kweilin. My friend from Nanking, she was so good to me. She bribed a man to steal a wheelbarrow used to haul coal. She promised to warn our other friends.

"I packed my things and my two babies into this wheelbarrow and began pushing to Chungking four days before the Japanese marched into Kweilin. On the road I heard news of the slaughter from people running past me. It was terrible. Up to the last day, the Kuomintang insisted that Kweilin was safe, protected by the Chinese army. But later that day, the streets of Kweilin were strewn with newspapers reporting great Kuomintang victories, and on top of these papers, like fresh fish from a butcher, lay rows of people—men, women, and children who had never lost hope, but had lost their lives instead.

When I heard this news, I walked faster and faster, asking myself at each step, Were they foolish? Were they brave?

"I pushed toward Chungking, until my wheel broke. I abandoned my beautiful mah jong table of *hong mu*. By then I didn't have enough feeling left in my body to cry. I tied scarves into slings and put a baby on each side of my shoulder. I carried a bag in each hand, one with clothes, the other with food. I carried these things until deep grooves grew in my hands. And I finally dropped one bag after the other when my hands began to bleed and became too slippery to hold onto anything.

"Along the way, I saw others had done the same, gradually given up hope. It was like a pathway inlaid with treasures that grew in value along the way. Bolts of fine fabric and books. Paintings of ancestors and carpenter tools. Until one could see cages of ducklings now quiet with thirst and, later still, silver urns lying in the road, where people had been too tired to carry them for any kind of future hope. By the time I arrived in Chungking I had lost everything except for three fancy silk dresses which I wore one on top of the other."

"What do you mean by 'everything'?" I gasped at the end. I was stunned to realize the story had been true all along. "What happened to the babies?"

She didn't even pause to think. She simply said in a way that made it clear there was no more to the story: "Your father is not my first husband. You are not those babies."

❧

Jing-mei goes to the Joy Luck Club meeting at Auntie An-mei's home. She and the three aunties play mah jong and talk. When the game ends, the aunties tell her not to leave. They have important news.

I sit down. Auntie An-mei leaves the room quickly and returns with a bowl of peanuts, then quietly shuts the door. Everybody is quiet, as if nobody knew where to begin.

It is Auntie Ying who finally speaks. "I think you mother die with an important thought on her mind," she says in halting English. And then she begins to speak in Chinese, calmly, softly.

"Your mother was a very strong woman, a good mother. She loved you very much, more than her own life. And that's why you can understand why a mother like this could never forget her other daughters. She knew they were alive, and before she died she wanted to find her daughters in China."

The babies in Kweilin, I think. I was not those babies. The babies in a sling on her shoulder. Her other daughters. And now I feel as if I were in Kweilin amidst the bombing and I can see these babies lying on the side of the road, their red thumbs popped out of their mouths, screaming to be reclaimed. Somebody took them away. They're safe. And now my mother's left me forever, gone back to China to get these babies. I can barely hear Auntie Ying's voice.

"She had searched for years, written letters back and forth," says Auntie Ying. "And last year she got an address. She was going to tell your father soon. Aii-ya, what a shame. A lifetime of waiting."

Auntie An-mei interrupts with an excited voice: "So your aunties and I, we wrote to this address," she says. "We say that a certain party, your mother, want to meet another certain party. And this party write back to us. They are your sisters, Jing-mei."

My sisters, I repeat to myself, saying these two words together for the first time.

Auntie An-mei is holding a sheet of paper as thin as wrapping tissue. In perfectly straight vertical rows I see Chinese characters written in blue fountain-pen ink. A word is smudged. A tear? I take the letter with shaking hands, marveling at how smart my sisters must be to be able to read and write Chinese.

The aunties are all smiling at me, as though I had been a dying person who has now miraculously recovered. Auntie Ying is handing me another envelope. Inside is a check made out to June Woo for $1,200. I can't believe it.

"My sisters are sending *me* money?" I ask.

"No, no," says Auntie Lin with her mock exasperated voice. "Every year we save our mah jong winnings for big banquet at fancy restaurant. Most times your mother win, so most is her money. We add just a little, so you can go Hong Kong, take a train to Shanghai, see your sisters. Besides, we all getting too rich, too fat." She pats her stomach for proof.

"See my sisters," I say numbly. I am awed by this prospect, trying to imagine what I would see. And I am embarrassed by the end-of-the-year-banquet lie my aunties have told to mask their generosity. I am crying now, sobbing and laughing at the same time, seeing but not understanding this loyalty to my mother.

"You must see your sisters and tell them about your mother's death," says Auntie Ying. "But most important, you must tell them about her life. The mother they did not know, they must now know."

"See my sisters, tell them about my mother," I say, nodding. "What will I say? What can I tell them about my mother? I don't know anything. She was my mother."

The aunties are looking at me as if I had become crazy right before their eyes.

"Not know your own mother?" cries Auntie An-mei with disbelief. "How can you say? Your mother is in your bones!"

"Tell them stories of your family here. How she became success," offers Auntie Lin.

"Tell them stories she told you, lessons she taught, what you know about her mind that has become your mind," says Auntie Ying. "You mother very smart lady."

I hear more choruses of "Tell them, tell them" as each Auntie frantically tries to think what should be passed on.

"Her kindness."

"Her smartness."

"Her dutiful nature to family."

"Her hopes, things that matter to her."

"The excellent dishes she cooked."

"Imagine, a daughter not knowing her own mother!"

And then it occurs to me. They are frightened. In me, they see their own daughters, just as ignorant, just as unmindful of all the truths and hopes they have brought to America. They see daughters who grow impatient when their mothers talk in Chinese, who think they are stupid when they explain things in fractured English. They see that joy and luck do not mean the same to their daughters, that to these closed American-born minds "joy luck" is not a word, it does not exist. They see daughters who will bear grandchildren born without any connecting hope passed from generation to generation.

"I will tell them everything," I say simply, and the aunties look at me with doubtful faces.

"I will remember everything about her and tell them," I say more firmly. And gradually, one by one, they smile and pat my hand. They still look troubled, as if something were out of balance. But they also look hopeful that what I say will become true. What more can they ask? What more can I promise?

Finally, Jing-mei and her father, Canning Woo, go to China to meet her half-sisters. First they fly from San Francisco to Hong Kong. There, they take a train to Guangzhou, where they will visit her father's aunt.

As the train crosses into China, Jing-mei feels different. "My mother was right," she thinks, "I am becoming Chinese." As they look at the Chinese land around them, both Jing-mei and her father have tears in their eyes.

Looking out the train window, Jing-mei recalls the rest of the events that led to this trip.

In less than three hours, we will be in Guangzhou, which my guidebook tells me is how one properly refers to Canton these days. It seems all the cities I have heard of, except Shanghai, have changed their spellings. I think they are saying China has changed in other ways as well. Chungking is Chongqing. And Kweilin is Guilin. I have looked these names up, because after we see my father's aunt in Guangzhou, we will catch a plane to Shanghai, where I will meet my two half-sisters for the first time.

They are my mother's twin daughters from her first marriage, little babies she was forced to abandon on a road as she was fleeing Kweilin for Chungking in 1944. That was all my mother had told me about these daughters, so they had remained babies in my mind, all these years, sitting on the side of a road, listening to bombs whistling in the distance while sucking their patient red thumbs.

And it was only this year that someone found them and wrote with this joyful news. A letter came from Shanghai, addressed to my mother. When I first heard about this, that they were alive, I imagined my identical sisters transforming from little babies into six-year-old girls. In my mind, they were seated next to each other at a table, taking turns with the fountain pen. One would write a neat row of characters: *Dearest Mama. We are alive.* She would brush back her wispy bangs and hand the other sister the pen, and she would write: *Come get us. Please hurry.*

Of course they could not know that my mother had died three months before, suddenly, when a blood vessel in her brain burst. One minute she was talking to my father, complaining about the tenants upstairs, scheming how to evict them under the pretense that relatives from China were moving in. The next minute she was holding her head, her eyes squeezed shut, groping for the sofa, and then crumpling softly to the floor with fluttering hands.

So my father had been the first one to open the letter, a long letter it turned out. And they did call her Mama. They said they always revered her as their true mother. They kept a framed picture of her. They told her about their life, from the time my mother last saw them on the road leaving Kweilin to when they were finally found.

And the letter had broken my father's heart so much—these daughters calling my mother from another life he never knew—that he gave the letter to my mother's old friend Auntie Lindo and asked her to write back and tell my sisters, in the gentlest way possible, that my mother was dead.

But instead Auntie Lindo took the letter to the Joy Luck Club and discussed with Auntie Ying and Auntie An-mei what should be done, because they had known for many years about my mother's search for her twin daughters, her endless hope. Auntie Lindo and the others cried over this double tragedy, of losing my mother three months before, and now again. And so they couldn't help but think of some miracle, some possible way of reviving her from the dead, so my mother could fulfill her dream.

So this is what they wrote to my sisters in Shanghai: "Dearest Daughters, I too have never forgotten you in my memory or in my heart. I never gave up hope that we would see each other again in a joyous reunion. I am only sorry it has been too long. I want to tell you everything about my life since I last saw you. I want to tell you this when our family comes to see you in China...." They signed it with my mother's name.

It wasn't until all this had been done that they first told me about my sisters, the letter they received, the one they wrote back.

"They'll think she's coming, then," I murmured. And I had imagined my sisters now being ten or eleven, jumping up and down, holding hands, their pigtails bouncing, excited that their mother—*their* mother—was coming, whereas my mother was dead.

"How can you say she is not coming in a letter?" said Auntie Lindo. "She is their mother. She is your mother. You must be the one to tell them. All these years, they have been dreaming of her." And I thought she was right.

But then I started dreaming, too, of my mother and my sisters and how it would be if I arrived in Shanghai. All these years, while they waited to be found, I had lived with my mother and then had lost her. I imagined seeing my sisters at the airport. They would be standing on their tiptoes, looking anxiously, scanning from one dark head to another as we got off the plane. And I would recognize them instantly, their faces with the identical worried look.

"*Jyejye, Jyejye.* Sister, Sister. We are here," I saw myself saying in my poor version of Chinese.

"Where is Mama?" they would say, and look around, still smiling, two flushed and eager faces. "Is she hiding?" And this would have been like my mother, to stand behind just a bit, to tease a little and make people's patience pull a little on their hearts. I would shake my head and tell my sisters she was not hiding.

"Oh, that must be Mama, no?" one of my sisters would whisper excitedly, pointing to another small woman completely engulfed in a tower of presents. And that, too, would have been like my mother, to bring mountains of gifts, food, and toys for children—all bought on sale—shunning thanks, saying the gifts were nothing, and later turning the labels over to show my sisters, "Calvin Klein, 100% wool."

I imagined myself starting to say, "Sisters, I am sorry, I have come alone . . ." and before I could tell them—they could see it in my face—they were wailing, pulling their hair, their lips twisted in pain, as they ran away from me. And then I saw myself getting back on the plane and coming home.

After I had dreamed this scene many times—watching their despair turn from horror into anger—I begged Auntie Lindo to write another letter. And at first she refused.

"How can I say she is dead? I cannot write this," said Auntie Lindo with a stubborn look.

"But it's cruel to have them believe she's coming on the plane," I said. "When they see it's just me, they'll hate me."

"Hate you? Cannot be." She was scowling. "You are their own sister, their only family."

"You don't understand," I protested.

"What I don't understand?" she said.

And I whispered, "They'll think I'm responsible, that she died because I didn't appreciate her."

And Auntie Lindo looked satisfied and sad at the same time, as if this were true and I had finally realized it. She sat down for an hour, and when she stood up she handed me a two-page letter. She had tears in her eyes. I realized that the very thing I had feared, she had done. So even if she had written the news of my mother's death in English, I wouldn't have had the heart to read it.

"Thank you," I whispered.

One evening, after they first arrive in China, Canning Woo tells Jing-mei more about her mother and her search for her children.

He explains how the babies were discovered by the side of the road. When Suyuan became too sick to carry them, she left them with her most precious possessions in hopes that someone would find them and care for them.

She put all her money and jewels under the shirt of one baby, and family photos under the shirt of the other. On the backs of the photos, she wrote the names of the girls. She left a note asking that the babies be taken care of and returned, for a reward, after the war.

Later Suyuan was found unconscious on the road and was taken by soldiers to a missionary hospital in Chungking. There she learned that her husband had died. This was where she met Canning Woo, who was also a patient in the same hospital.

Suyuan tried to find her daughters for several years, but then she had to leave China for America. For 30 years, Suyuan could not write or call China to find out about her daughters. That is because the 1949 Communist takeover in China ended official relations between the United States and China. She could not begin to look for her daughters until the 1970s, when the United States officially recognized China again.

It was an old peasant woman who found them. "How could I resist?" the peasant woman later told your sisters when they were older. They were still sitting obediently near where your mother had left them, looking like little fairy queens waiting for their sedan to arrive.

The woman, Mei Ching, and her husband, Mei Han, lived in a stone cave. There were thousands of hidden caves like that in and around Kweilin so secret that the people remained hidden even after the war ended. The Meis would come out of their cave every few days and forage for food supplies left on the road, and sometimes they would see something that they both agreed was a tragedy to leave behind. So one day they took back to their cave a delicately painted set of rice bowls, another day a little footstool with a velvet cushion and two new wedding blankets. And once, it was your sisters.

They were pious people, Muslims, who believed the twin babies were a sign of double luck, and they were sure of this when, later in the evening, they discovered how valuable the babies were. She and her husband had never seen rings and bracelets like those. And while they admired the pictures, knowing the babies came from a good family, neither of them could read or write. It was not until many months later that Mei Ching found someone who could read the writing on the back. By then, she loved these baby girls like her own.

In 1952 Mei Han, the husband, died. The twins were already eight years old, and Mei Ching now decided it was time to find your sisters' true family.

She showed the girls the picture of their mother and told them they had been born into a great family and she would take them back to see their true mother and grandparents. Mei Ching told them about the reward, but she swore she would refuse it. She loved these girls so much, she only wanted them to have what they were entitled to—a better life, a fine house, educated ways. Maybe the family would let her stay on as the girls' amah. Yes, she was certain they would insist.

Of course, when she found the place at 9 Weichang Lu, in the old French Concession, it was something completely different. It was the site of a factory building, recently constructed, and none of the workers knew what had become of the family whose house had burned down on that spot.

Mei Ching could not have known, of course, that your mother and I, her new husband, had already returned to that same place in 1945 in hopes of finding both her family and her daughters.

Your mother and I stayed in China until 1947. We went to many different cities—back to Kweilin, to Changsha, as far south as Kunming. She was always looking out of one corner of her eye for twin babies, then little girls. Later we went to Hong Kong, and when we finally left in 1949 for the United States, I think she was even looking for them on the boat. But when we arrived, she no longer talked about them. I thought, At last, they have died in her heart.

When letters could be openly exchanged between China and the United States, she wrote immediately to old friends in Shanghai and Kweilin. I did not know she did this. Auntie Lindo told me. But of course, by then, all the street names had changed. Some people had died, others had moved away. So it took many years to find a contact. And when she did find an old schoolmate's address and wrote asking her to look for her daughters, her friend wrote back and said this was impossible, like looking for a needle on the bottom of the ocean. How did she know her daughters were in Shanghai and not somewhere else in China? The friend, of course, did not ask, How do you know your daughters are still alive?

So her schoolmate did not look. Finding babies lost during the war was a matter of foolish imagination, and she had no time for that.

But every year, your mother wrote to different people. And this last year, I think she got a big idea in her head, to go to China and find them herself. I remember she told me, "Canning, we should go, before it is too late, before we are too old." And I told her we were already too old, it was already too late.

I just thought she wanted to be a tourist! I didn't know she wanted to go and look for her daughters. So when I said it was too late, that must have put a terrible thought in her head that her daughters might be dead. And I think this possibility grew bigger and bigger in her head, until it killed her.

Maybe it was your mother's dead spirit who guided her Shanghai schoolmate to find her daughters. Because after your mother died, the schoolmate saw your sisters, by chance, while shopping for shoes at the Number One

Department Store on Nanjing Dong Road. She said it was like a dream, seeing these two women who looked so much alike, moving down the stairs together. There was something about their facial expressions that reminded the schoolmate of your mother.

She quickly walked over to them and called their names, which of course, they did not recognize at first, because Mei Ching had changed their names. But your mother's friend was so sure, she persisted. "Are you not Wang Chwun Yu and Wang Chwun Hwa?" she asked them. And then these double-image women became very excited, because they remembered the names written on the back of an old photo, a photo of a young man and woman they still honored, as their much-loved first parents, who had died and become spirit ghosts still roaming the earth looking for them.

At last, Jing-mei and her father take a plane to Shanghai to meet her two half-sisters.

"Wake up, we're here," says my father. And I awake with my heart pounding in my throat. I look out the window and we're already on the runway. It's gray outside.

And now I'm walking down the steps of the plane, onto the tarmac and toward the building. If only, I think, if only my mother had lived long enough to be the one walking toward them. I am so nervous I cannot even feel my feet. I am just moving somehow.

Somebody shouts, "She's arrived!" And then I see her. Her short hair. Her small body. And that same look on her face. She has the back of her hand pressed hard against her mouth. She is crying as though she had gone through a terrible ordeal and were happy it is over.

And I know it's not my mother, yet it is the same look she had when I was five and had disappeared all afternoon, for such a long time, that she was convinced I was dead. And when I miraculously appeared, sleepy-eyed, crawling from underneath my bed, she wept and laughed, biting the back of her hand to make sure it was true.

And now I see her again, two of her, waving, and in one hand there is a photo, the Polaroid I sent them. As soon as I get beyond the gate, we run toward each other, all three of us embracing, all hesitations and expectations forgotten.

"Mama, Mama," we all murmur, as if she is among us.

My sisters look at me, proudly. *"Meimei jandale,"* says one sister proudly to the other. "Little Sister has grown up." I look at their faces again and I see no trace of my mother in them. Yet they still look familiar. And now I also see what part of me is Chinese. It is so obvious. It is my family. It is in our blood. After all these years, it can finally be let go.

My sisters and I stand, arms around each other, laughing and wiping the tears from each other's eyes. The flash of the Polaroid goes off and my father hands me the snapshot. My sisters and I watch quietly together, eager to see what develops.

The gray-green surface changes to the bright colors of our three images, sharpening and deepening all at once. And although we don't speak, I know we all see it: Together we look like our mother. Her same eyes, her same mouth, open in surprise to see, at last, her long-cherished wish.

MAPS OF PLACES MENTIONED IN THE SELECTIONS

Today, Kweilin is called Guilin; Chungking is called Chongqing Canton is called Guangzhou; Peking is called Beijing and Nanking is called Nanjing.

Questions for the Reader

❖

Thinking About the Story

1. What was interesting for you about the selections from *The Joy Luck Club*?

2. What do you think about the relationship between Jing-mei and her mother? What do the selections tell you about their feelings for each other?

3. What are some things that you learned about Chinese family life from these selections? How is it similar to any kind of family life?

4. From the story the mother tells, what kind of person do you think she is? How do you feel about her leaving her two babies by the side of the road?

5. What do you think were the most important things Amy Tan wanted to say in the selections?

6. In what ways did the selections answer the questions you had before you began reading or listening?

7. Were any parts of the selections difficult to understand? If so, you may want to read or listen to them again. Discuss with your learning partners possible reasons why they were difficult.

Thinking About the Writing

1. These selections tell two stories. One is Jing-mei's story about her relationship with her mother. The other story is Suyuan's story about the war and losing and then trying to find her two babies. One story fits into another. How does Amy Tan keep you interested in both stories?

2. In these selections different characters tell different parts of the story. Another way a writer could have done this would be to have just *one* person tell that story. Why do you think Amy Tan chose to have different people tell the story?

3. How did Amy Tan help you see, hear and feel what happened in the selections? Find the words, phrases or sentences that did this best.

4. Writers think carefully about their stories' settings, characters and events. In writing

these selections, which of these things do you think Amy Tan felt was most important? Find the parts of the story that support your opinion.

5. In the selections, Amy Tan uses dialogue. Dialogue can make a story more alive. Besides telling the reader what the characters said, the dialogue helps to bring out the personalities of the characters. Pick out some dialogue that you feel is strong, and explain how it helps the story.

6. Amy Tan, through her writing, makes us understand Jing-mei's complicated feelings about her mother. Find some parts in the selections that helped you understand this.

Activities

1. Were there any words that were difficult for you in the selections from *The Joy Luck Club*? Go back to these words and try to figure out their meanings. Discuss what you think each word means and why you made that guess. Look them up in a dictionary and see if your definitions are the same or different.

   Discuss with your learning partners how you are going to remember each word. Some ways to remember words are to put them on file cards, write them in a journal or create a personal dictionary. Be sure to use the words in your writing in a way that will help you to remember their meanings.

2. Talking with other people about what you have read can increase your understanding. Discussion can help you organize your thoughts, get new ideas and rethink your original ideas. Discuss your thoughts about the selections from *The Joy Luck Club* with someone else who has read them. Find out if you helped yourselves understand the selections in the same or different ways. Find out if your opinions about the selections are the same or different. See if your thoughts change as a result of this discussion.

3. After you finish reading or listening, you might want to write down your thoughts about the book. You could write your reflections on the book in a journal, or you could write about topics the book has brought up that you want to explore further. You could write a book review or a letter to a friend about the book.

4. Did reading the selections give you any ideas for your own writing? You might want to write about:

- how your thoughts and feelings toward your parents or grandparents changed as you grew older.
- how your heritage shapes your life.
- the complicated relationships between parents and children.

5. Sometimes organizing information in a visual way can help you better understand or remember it. Look at the chronology of world events and Jing-mei's family history on pages 62 and 63. You might want to make a similar chronology for your family.

6. If you could talk to Amy Tan, what questions would you ask about her writing? You might want to write the questions in a journal.

7. Interview someone you know about how they came to America. Find out how this experience affected their relationships with other people in their family.

8. These selections describe a way food is believed to bring good luck in the Chinese culture. In your culture, what are some foods or other things that bring good luck? You may want to write about them. You may want to bring one of these foods to class to share with your learning partners.

Glossary

❂

butong. Not the same thing.

chabudwo. Almost the same thing.

chr. A play in mah jong.

dyansyin. Foods that bring good luck, usually served in small amounts at lunch time.

hong mu. Chinese red wood.

jandale. She has grown up.

jyejye. Older sister.

Kuomintang. A major political party in China from 1928–1949. Also known as the Nationalist Party.

mah jong. An old Chinese game that uses a set of small tiles with Chinese drawings and symbols. It is played somewhat like bridge.

meimei. Younger sister.

Nanjing Dong Road. An important road in Shanghai.

pai. Mah jong tiles. There are at least 136 mah jong tiles to a game set.

pung. A play in mah jong.

yuan. Dollar. The basic unit of Chinese currency.

About Amy Tan

❖

Amy Tan was born in 1952 in Oakland, California. Her father came to America from China in 1947, her mother in 1949. Her father was a Baptist minister and electrical engineer. Her mother was a vocational nurse.

Amy Tan went to college and graduate school at San Jose State University in San Jose, California. Her parents wanted her to become a doctor and a pianist. Instead, she studied English and linguistics.

After college, she worked as a consultant to programs for disabled children. Later she became a freelance writer. She wrote speeches and articles for business executives and articles about the business world.

She also went to weekly creative writing classes. In these classes, she began to write short stories about Chinese mothers and daughters. She wove these together to make *The Joy Luck Club*. It was her first book of fiction. Her classmates made suggestions that helped her to writing. In the acknowledgements to *The Joy Luck Club,* she thanks the members of her writers' group for their "kindness and criticism."

Amy Tan has written two other books of fiction. They are called *The Kitchen God's Wife* and *The Hundred Secret Senses.*

Tan lives with her husband, Lou DeMattei, in San Francisco, where parts of *The Joy Luck Club* are set.

About Modern China

❖

Many of the events in the selections from *The Joy Luck Club* take place in China. They occur during two different times in China's recent history—during China's war with Japan from 1937 to 1945, and, years later, when American tourists went to China in the 1980s.

The Chinese have an ancient culture and a very developed civilization. The history of China goes back nearly 5,000 years.

China has always had a large population. Most people live in the countryside and work on farms. Today China has a population of about one billion people. About two-thirds of China is mountains and desert. Almost all the people live in the eastern third of the country.

China Under the Dynasties

For most of its history, China was ruled by dynasties. A dynasty is a powerful family that passes leadership down through generations.

The last dynasty to rule China was started by once-nomadic people from Manchuria, called the Manchus. They controlled China for almost 300 years, from 1644 until 1912.

In the period of the dynasties, life for the average person was hard. Most people had no right to own land and almost everyone lived in poverty. They had no legal rights. Women had low status and were often mistreated. With so many people and so little cultivated land, there wasn't always enough food.

Modern China

In the 1600s, the first traders from Europe came to China to bring its tea and silk back to their countries. By the late 1800s, Westerners gained control of all trade going in and out of China. They made the Chinese agree to trade deals that favored Westerners. Westerners enforced these unfair deals with their more advanced weapons and technology.

Some Chinese felt that the Manchu emperor was corrupt and not doing enough to modernize China. In 1911, a revolution overthrew the rule of the Manchu emperor. The Republic of China was established.

Communists and Nationalists

After this revolution, there was still poverty and conflict in China. Two political groups started at this time: the Nationalists and the Communists. The Communists thought all of China's people should share the nation's farmland and industry. They thought that the economy should be run by a strong central government. They were supported by the Marxists of Russia.

The Nationalist Party (or the Kuomintang) wanted to model China on the Western democracies. They wanted a market economy, where people ran their own businesses. They were supported by the United States and some European countries.

At first the two Chinese political groups worked together, but they soon became enemies. By the 1930s, the Nationalists and the Communists controlled separate parts of the country. The two groups were at war with each other.

War With Japan

Japan had been an enemy of China for a long time. War-torn China in the 1930s became easy prey for the powerful Japanese army. The

Japanese had occupied parts of China since 1905. They grew more aggressive in the 1930s. In 1937, Japan began bombing outside the Chinese city of Peking (now spelled Beijing). This was the beginning of World War II in Asia. Over the next year, Japan took control of most of eastern China. Both the Nationalists and the Communists fought against the Japanese.

The war caused great poverty and high inflation in China. There was famine because the country's resources were used for the army and because farmland was destroyed in the fighting. Many homes were destroyed. People fled the advancing Japanese army.

China's war with Japan continued until 1945. Hundreds of thousands, perhaps millions, of Chinese died. The other Allied forces (United States, England, France, Soviet Union) who were fighting Japan in World War II gave China aid.

China Under Communist Rule

After Japan was defeated in 1945, the Nationalists and Communists turned on each other. In 1949, under Mao Tse-tung's leadership, the Communists defeated the Nationalists and took power. The Nationalist leader Chiang Kai-shek and his army fled to Formosa (later known as Taiwan), an island off the coast of China.

Many Chinese who did not want to live under Communist rule also fled to Taiwan, and some moved to the United States, Canada and other countries.

The Break With the West

The United States and other Western countries did not officially "recognize" the Communist government in Mainland China as the government of China. Instead, they treated the Nationalist government on the island of Taiwan as the official government of China. Communist China and the Western countries remained hostile to each other for many years.

For Chinese who had left China to live in other countries, it was hard to find out what was going on in China—people could not exchange letters to get the news.

The years after the 1949 revolution brought great change in China. The Chinese Communist government tried to rebuild the country. Industry and farmland were put under government control. Some things improved under the Communists: people had more to eat and more people learned how to read and write. But life was still hard for the average person. People who disagreed with the government were punished. And even with changes, China was still a poor country.

But in the 1970s, Chinese leaders decided to start to talk with the West. In 1972, the American president, Richard Nixon, went to China and met with Mao Tse-tung. After Nixon's visit, a limited amount of tourism began between the two countries. In 1979, China and the United States agreed to let trade go back and forth between their countries.

This event was greeted with joy by Chinese living in the United States. They could now get in touch with their friends and relatives in China.

In the late 1980s, the ties between China and the West became weaker. There were conflicts in China again about personal freedoms. People demonstrated against political corruption. In the 1989 student-led demonstrations in Tiananmen Square, many demonstrators were killed.

The history of China in the last sixty years has been one of great change. China has had different governments and leaders, from emperors, to presidents to Communist Party leaders. Change is still happening in modern China, but in the early 1990s it remains the most powerful Communist country in the world.

About Mah Jong

✿

The women of the Joy Luck Club play an old Chinese game called mah jong. Mah jong is played somewhat like a card game. Instead of using a deck of cards, mah jong uses a set of rectangular tiles or *pai*. *Pai* were usually made of ivory and bamboo. Modern sets are often made of plastic. There are at least 136 basic tiles. Each tile has traditional markings.

In the Joy Luck Club, there are four mah jong players. The game is played on a square table, usually covered with a cloth or pad to soften the clicking noise of the moving tiles. The players sit at the four sides or corners of the table.

Players call out when they collect certain tiles. *Pung!* means having three tiles of the same number in the same suit. *Chr!* means having a run of three tiles of the same suit.

Mah jong players often put money into a "kitty" before the game. The winning player can claim the kitty. For more information about mah jong in the United States, write to: The National Mah Jong League, 250 West 57 Street, New York, NY 10019.

Chronology of Events

World History	Year	Jing-mei's Family History
World History Japan bombs Peking and starrs WWII. China is at war with Japan.	1937	
	1937–1945	Suyuan goes to Kweilin to be safe during the war. She starts the first Joy Luck Club.
World War II between the Allies (United States, England, France, Soviet Union and China) and the Axis (Germany, Italy, and Japan).	1941–1945	
	1944–1945	Suyuan Woo flees from Kweilin to Chungking. Along the way she must leave her two daughters on the road. Suyuan's first husband dies. Suyuan marries Canning Woo. They search for her missing children.
Civil war in China between the Chinese Communists and the Nationalists	1946–1949	

	Republic of China is established. Diplomatic relations between the United States and the People's Republic of China are broken. Suyuan and Canning Woo move to San Francisco. Suyuan starts the second Joy Luck Club.
1951	Jing-mei "June" Woo is born in San Francisco, California.
1971	The United Nations recognizes the People's Republic of China (formerly known as Red China or Mainland China).
1972	President Nixon visits China. Limited diplomatic relations between the United States and China resume.
1976	Communist leader Mao Tse-tung dies.
1979	The United States and the People's Republic of China start normal diplomatic relations. Suyuan writes letters to China searching for her lost daughters.
1987	Suyuan Woo dies. The missing daughters write from China. Jing-mei Woo and Canning Woo go to China to see their family.